Men's Training Class

BY JARROD JACOBS

© 2018 Jacobs Publications
All rights reserved. No part of this book may be reproduced in any form without written permission of the publisher.

Published by:
Jacobs Publications
5695 Caneyville Rd.
Morgantown, KY 42261

Printed in the United States of America

ISBN-13: 978-1717185051
ISBN-10: 1717185053

Supplemental Material Available:
Men's Training Class (Teacher's Edition)

Table Of Contents

Introduction 5
Lesson 1 – "Stage Fright" 7
Lesson 2 – "Reading Scripture" 11
Lesson 3 – "Leading Songs" 17
Lesson 4 – "Offering Prayer" 23
Lesson 5 – "The Lord's Supper & Collection" ... 29
Lesson 6 – "Making A Short Talk" 33
Conclusion 37
Extra Material 38

Introduction

The purpose of these lessons is to help men become confident in leading the congregation in the public worship of the church. Since God wants us to worship Him *"in spirit and in truth"* (Jn. 4:24), and has given us specific instructions on how we are to worship Him (Acts 2:42, 20:7; Eph. 5:19; I Cor. 16:1-2; etc.) then, by implication, it is necessary for men to help in conducting this worship. God expects things to be done *"decently and in order"* (I Cor. 14:33). Thus, we need men to lead us in worship in the manner God demands.

Yet, when men are asked to take part in leading the congregation in worship, some feel inadequate and incapable of doing the job. Fear gets in the way and can be an obstacle to doing what God expects.

Question: Why might men feel afraid to take part in a public leading role in the worship? _____
_____
_____

Have you ever felt inadequate, or uneasy about serving in a public manner? What made you feel like this? Could it be because you were unfamiliar with what was expected? Could it be you were afraid of folks looking at you? Could it be you were concerned you might somehow "fail" at the duty? Maybe all of these fears crossed your mind?

Rest assured, all men who have served publicly have had these same fears and concerns. However, folks overcame their fears, and you can overcome your fear as well. If you have these fears, this class is for you! We will deal with some of the fears and prove that we can overcome them.

If you do not have these fears, but want to simply learn more and gain more experience, then this class is for you! We will take time to go through all the acts of worship and the things necessary for serving God acceptably *"in spirit and in truth."*

Some Suggestions For This Class:

1. Bring your Bible, some writing utensil, and paper for taking notes. Or, feel free to take notes in your book if you prefer. Take notes freely if this will help you in the learning process.

2. Be yourself! Don't be afraid to make mistakes, because we all WILL do it! Mistakes can be stepping-stones to make us better if we will allow it!

3. Do your best! You will have some work to do and times when you are "on-your-feet" in every class. Don't be scared and don't waste time in class. Be a *willing* participant. We are all on the same team! Therefore, let us all do our best and encourage each other.

4. Remember, you are serving GOD by making this effort to better yourself. Seek to please Him in all you do.

5. Please remember that any criticism that is given is done with love and concern that we might be better. Take it that way!

6. Please take what we learn in each class and use it ASAP! Don't wait for the end of the session to start applying what you learn. Apply it at the next opportunity you have to serve publicly.

Lesson 1: Stage Fright

For lack of a better term, we will call the fear one has of standing in front of people in a worship service "stage fight." Stage fright is defined as: "nervousness felt at appearing before an audience" (Webster's). While we recognize that our worship time is not actually "appearing before an audience" since we are all participating, it is still true that people become nervous when they feel like everyone's eyes are on them.

Sometimes, when people get nervous like this, they will feel sick. Some want to run away. Others may "freeze up" and feel like they cannot move, or they lose their train of thought. Others may laugh or cry uncontrollably.

<u>Other symptoms of stage fright include:</u>
- Shortness of breath.
- Repeatedly licking lips.
- High pitch in the voice.
- Extreme tension.
- Forgetting what one planned to say.
- Trembling/Shaking in knees, legs, or hands.
- Dry mouth/throat.
- "Butterflies" in the stomach.
- Pounding of the heart.
- Cold sweat.

Please remember *everyone experiences this from time to time!* If you experience these things, you are not alone! There is a cure!

Overcoming Stage Fright

How does one overcome this problem? The answer is quite simple: *relax* and *face your fear!* Before you convince yourself that relaxing is an impossible task, please remember that everyone has had this feeling, and many people in the past have overcome it! You can as well!

What are some key points to remember in order to overcome stage fright?

1. Pray about it (I Thess. 5:17). Talk to God about the situation. Pour your heart out to Him, telling Him you want to do this work, and ask Him to give you the opportunity as well as the bravery to do it. Remember what Paul said in Philippians 4:13.

2. Remember that talking to a large group is no different than a small group, or a single person. This room may be filled with individuals, but if you imagine you are talking to just one person in the room, this can sometimes help calm you.

3. Remember that no one here is against you! We all want you to succeed and do well. You are helping us in our worship, and therefore, we are on your side!

4. One good way to relax is to remember to ***breathe!*** Many people forget to breathe when nervous, and they tense up even more. Breathe naturally, and deeply. Relax the shoulders and be ready to help the congregation to worship God!

5. One of the best ways to relax and overcome stage fright is to have experience! In other words, do it! Do not let fears get in the way, but make the earnest effort. Once you have done this the first time, future efforts become much easier. Experience builds confidence. Progress will come every time you try to lead the congregation in a public manner. You may not realize it, but progress is happening! Remember: If you never try, you will never succeed!

Fear is only a state of mind. Usually, men fear the unknown more than anything else. After one time of serving in a public manner, however, it is no longer "unknown"! Let us be ready to take that first step to help lead the congregation in worship. Action will help conquer your stage fright!

Questions:

1. What are the five acts of worship? What Scripture(s) prove this?

2. What do you think gives you the greatest fear when leading in worship?

3. What do you think you can do to conquer this fear? (Hint: "Nothing" is the wrong answer!)

"On-Your-Feet"

Be ready to lead one verse of a song in class. (You can choose the song.)

Be ready to lead a prayer.

Be ready to read Scripture.

Lesson 2:
Reading Scripture

When we worship God, we will spend time reading from the Scriptures. This is central in our services. Think about our Sunday AM class time and worship for a moment. When will we read Scriptures during those times? _____
_____
When will we read Scriptures on Sunday PM? _____
_____
When will we read Scriptures on Wednesday night? _____
_____

If we are going to help in the public part of worship, then we need to be ready to read the Scriptures publicly. This is something we find folks doing in Old Testament days. For example, we see Moses reading Scriptures (Ex. 24:7). Joshua read the Scriptures (Josh. 8:34-35). Ezra and the Levites read from God's book (Neh. 8:8-12).

Not only do we find folks in Old Testament days reading Scriptures in a public way, but we see this occurring in the New Testament! Jesus read the Scriptures publicly (Lk. 4:16-20). The Colossians read God's word in a public manner, too (Col. 4:16). The Thessalonians did the same (I Thess. 5:27). Therefore, when we take part in a public reading of the Scriptures, we are doing something that has been done for thousands of years!

The Bible is a book that is meant to be read aloud to others. We know the Eunuch read God's word for others to hear (Acts 8:27-30). I Timothy 4:13 speaks about the need for Timothy to give himself to "reading." Some Bible versions emphasize the fact that the "reading" in this passage was public reading. For example:

- (Common English Version) Until I arrive, be sure to keep on **_reading the Scriptures in worship_**, and don't stop preaching and teaching.
- (English Majority-Text Version) Until I come, give attention to **_public reading_**, to exhortation, to doctrine.
- (Easy-To-Read Version) Continue to **_read the Scriptures to the people_**, encourage them, and teach them. Do this until I come.
- (English Standard Version) Until I come, devote yourself to the **_public reading of Scripture_**, to exhortation, to teaching.
- (Good News Bible) Until I come, give your time and effort to the **_public reading of the Scriptures_** and to preaching and teaching.
- (God's Word) Until I get there, concentrate on **_reading Scripture in worship_**, giving encouraging messages, and teaching people.
- (International Standard Version) Until I arrive, give your full concentration to **_the public reading of Scripture_**, to exhorting, and to teaching.
- (Lexham English Bible) Until I come, pay attention to **_the public reading_**, to exhortation, to teaching.
- (Tree of Life Version) Until I come, devote yourself to **_the public reading of Scripture_**, to encouragement, and to teaching.
- (Williams New Testament) Until I come, devote yourself to **_the public reading of the Scriptures_**, and to preaching and teaching.

Why ought we read the Scriptures publicly? It is because through reading the Scriptures, folks are able to understand (Eph. 4:3)! Just think: In our public reading, we are trying to help folks to understand God's will! What a privilege!

Pointers For Effective Reading

If we want to be effective readers in public, then let us consider some sound advice that will help us in this work.

Read the passage a time or two before you read it publicly. Make sure you know all the words in the passage. If you have trouble pronouncing a word, then look it up, or ask someone to help you. Don't be ashamed to ask for help! We all need help from time to time in this!

Read so as to be heard. Nothing is worse than having someone read publicly, and when they do, they speak softly or mumble, and we cannot understand the words! Don't do this. Speak out! Speak up! Speak with confidence!

Learn to control your speech. This means:
- Control the speed with which you read. Familiarity with the text you are reading will help this (See first suggestion above.). Beware of reading too slowly or too quickly! Either extreme can be hard for those listening to the Bible being read during our public worship times!

    Ex. #1:
    Itdoesnothelppeopleunderstandthetextifwereadsoquicklythey cannotdistinguishonewordfromtheother!

    Ex. #2:
    It   does   not   help   our understanding   if   the   text   is read   too   slowly!

- Control the tone. Some are very monotone when reading. Remember, that we are reading the words/speeches of folks in various times in life. Do we speak monotone when angry? Happy? Sad? Joyous? Excited? Scared? Familiarity with the text we are reading helps us with our reading. Do not read in a monotone fashion.

- Use good eye contact. While reading, look up and engage those who are listening. Folks may be reading along, but they look up from time to time, and you need to do the same. If you are afraid of losing your place, put your index finger on the line in the Bible so you can look up and then look back down and continue reading.

Observe punctuation! We understand that punctuation was not in the original text, but it is in our Bibles, now. Let's observe punctuation. Stopping where there is a period (.), pausing where there is a comma (,) and using the correct inflection in the voice when there is a question mark (?) can mean a great deal to understanding the passage we are reading. Read I Timothy 4:12-16. Observe the punctuation. What do you see in this passage? How would it help our understanding when we observe the punctuation?
_____
_____
_____

Questions

1. What do you see as a benefit when you hear someone reading Scriptures to you?

2. What do you see as a hindrance when you hear someone reading Scriptures to you?

"On-Your-Feet"

Read John 19:10-11 to the class. Observe the punctuation. Should these verses be read with the same inflection in the voice? How should they be read?

Read Ephesians 6:1-4 to the class. Observe the punctuation. What happens when we respect the placement of the commas in this section?

Read Matthew 9:11-12 to the class. Observe the punctuation. When we do, can we not see that the words of the Pharisees will sound different than the words of Christ?

Lesson 3: Leading Songs

Another aspect of worship is singing praises to the God of Heaven (Col. 3:16; Eph. 5:19; I Cor. 14:15). Singing is something that is special. It requires a blending of words, a song, and the heart of man. Truly, we sing *"with the heart"* to God. An expedient way to do this is by having a male Christian lead us in song in a way that is *"decently and in order"* in our worship (I Cor. 14:40). Song leaders take their place with men who lead in congregational prayer, those who lead in our study of God's word (preacher/teacher), and those who lead our minds at the Lord's Supper so as to partake in a way pleasing to God. It is this outpouring of praise, love, and devotion, as well as anticipation of seeing God one day, that motivates our singing.

Our singing is intended to be another aspect of teaching (Col. 3:16). A song leader is leading the people in instruction as well as in song! It is not uncommon for some song leaders to remind the people to think carefully about the words in the songs they sing. This is because we are *"teaching and admonishing one another"* as we sing. This is not a "talent show," nor a time of entertainment. Songs are not something we do to "kill time" or break up some supposed "monotony" between the Lord's Supper and preaching or prayers or reading. Our songs are a part of our worship (Jn. 4:24). Paul said he would *"sing with the spirit and sing with the understanding"* (I Cor. 14:15). We need to have this as our goal every time we lead songs! Leading songs is very important. Below are helpful pointers in song leading, and some suggestions for those wishing to "keep time" while leading songs.

Pointers For Leading Congregational Singing Effectively.

Song leading is an important skill that can make an enormous difference in the way a congregation sings. There are a number of qualities that are important for success:

1. Having enthusiasm for singing.
2. Being able to establish a good rapport with the congregation.
3. Being comfortable with your own voice.
4. Being excited.

These attributes will help ensure a good singing experience for both the leader and the congregation.

Song leaders use a variety of approaches when leading the congregation, and no single approach or style is "right". What is important is to develop a style that is unique to your own personality and comfort level. The following are some things to consider:

- **Energy And Enthusiasm**

Probably nothing affects your success as a song leader as much as your own energy and enthusiasm. People respond to those who love what they do because enthusiasm is contagious. Those in the congregation who already enjoy singing will become even more enthusiastic. Those who are reluctant, or feel they can't sing, will want to be a part of this positive energy because of the song leader. The more encouragement they get from the leader, the better they will sing. The better they sing, the more confident they become, and the more willing to try new things. Take joy in this work and be at ease, as you lead songs.

- **Building Rapport**

Much of what you accomplish as a song leader will be the result of the kind of rapport you build with the congregation, and much of this depends on creating an environment conducive to singing. This means building trust by creating a safe place where people can sing what they know with gusto, and attempt what they don't know with eagerness and determination. Be open, be friendly, be accepting, and **remember to make eye contact**. The more folks can relate to you as a leader, the better they will sing.

- **Vocal Delivery**

It's important that you feel comfortable with your own voice so the congregation can relax and simply try to emulate what you're doing.

They will copy you, so be sure to be as accurate as possible, and model the kind of vocal production you're after. It shouldn't be a singing lesson, but if you demonstrate clearly, they can pick up many nuances without your ever having to formally "teach" them.

Some Techniques That Apply To All Songs:

- Careful Preparation

Make sure you know the song really well. Don't rely on the people to help "lead" the song. That's your job!

- Establish Tempo

In addition to getting the right starting note, a clean entry also means that the group knows ahead of time what the tempo will be. So, as you give the starting note, you should also indicate the tempo in some way, usually by using a hand gesture (See charts below). Once the song is started, it's important to maintain the tempo in a way that feels natural to you. A song's tempo is in many ways its most important element. If a group happens to sing off key, or scrambles the words, all is not lost. Once they lose the tempo, they lose the song!

- Modeling Good Singing

You do need to be able to use your voice in a way that's both authentic and accurate. The following are some qualities worth nurturing:

1. Clarity – The congregation needs to be able to hear and understand you. Sing out!
2. Conviction – They will pick up your energy (or lack thereof) immediately.
3. Correct Key – "Pitching" a song too high or too low is not helpful when we are singing. Using a pitch pipe or some other tuning device will be helpful if you are unsure of the key.

Above all, it's the love of the Lord and singing praise that is most important to convey. It's contagious!

Some ways in which one can "keep time" in a song are below. If the time signature in the song says ...

4/4 =

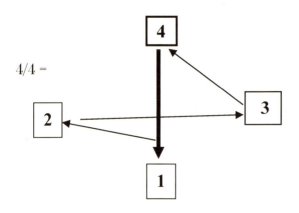

3/4 =

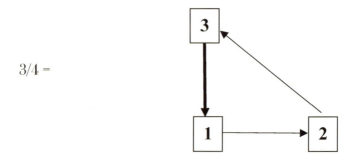

6/8 =

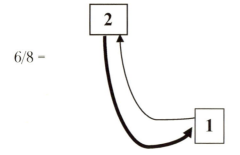

(Note: The **bolded arrow** is the "downbeat.")

Lastly, remember that when leading songs, you are trying to help the congregation sing this song *"decently and in order."* This cannot happen if there is general confusion as to what song you are leading. Remember to be courteous when leading and use some "tools" at your disposal to help folks.

1. When announcing songs, do it a couple of different ways. Example: "Our next song will be number 15, number 1-5." (Doing this will ensure folks did not think you announce song #50!)
2. Announce the number, and then the title of the song. This will help eliminate confusion with the congregation. In this case, you might announce the song number, the title, and the number again before beginning the song.
3. Make sure you post your songs on the board. Unless there is some emergency where you are leading for someone else at the last minute, you should always be here early enough to post your song numbers.

Brother Richard Stevens said the following about leading songs: "The first qualification for song leading should not be how well does he sing but how much Bible does he know, since he is choosing scriptural songs (Col. 3:16; Eph. 5:19). The second qualification should be how faithful is he, since he is leading songs before the brethren (II Cor. 3:2). The third qualification should be that he understands that he is a 'song leader' helping the congregation to sing together (an expedient to carry out the command to sing), and not a 'lead singer' using the congregation to back up his great singing (an addition to the command). And then with a faithful life, Bible knowledge, and an understanding of his role, he is on his way in the spiritual endeavor of leading songs of truth for the brethren."

Questions

1. What purpose does the song leader serve in the worship?

2. What verse(s) in the New Testament authorize us to sing praises to God?

3. Think of a song leader that really impressed you as a leader. What good qualities did he have that you can duplicate?

"On-Your-Feet"

Be ready to lead a song using the tips we have discussed above.

Trying "keeping time" with your hand. If you feel you are not coordinated enough, then set the songbook down on the stand and lead the song.

Lesson 4:
Offering Prayer

Prayer is offered every time we come together. It is our custom here to have an "opening" and "dismissal" prayer, as well as prayers during our time together. It is important that we know how to offer prayers publicly, and how each prayer needs to be *appropriate* to what is happening in the assembly.

What is prayer? _____
_____

Name the types of prayers that are often offered when we are together. _____
_____

As we begin this study, remember that our relationship before God makes a huge impact on whether or not our prayers are heard! Remember that God says He listens to the prayers of the righteous (I Pet. 3:10-12; Prov. 28:9). He is not listening to prayers offered by sinners, nor by Christians who are practicing sin (ex. I Pet. 3:7)! When leading a public prayer, be mindful of your personal standing before God (II Cor. 13:5)! Are you living in a manner that you are pleasing to God?

Sometimes, when men are asked to lead the congregation in a public prayer, they will feel intimidated about doing so. As we study this subject together, I hope this lesson will help us feel less intimidated and ready to lead the congregation in prayer when asked.

Perhaps part of the reason someone might feel intimidated is that he feels like he can't think of anything to say. In a prayer, we could lead the congregation to pray for:

- The sick (Jas. 5:15-16)
- The lost (Rom. 10:1)
- Our government leaders (I Tim. 2:1-2)
- Forgiveness of sins (Acts 8:22-23)
- Intercession for others = pray for someone else (enemy, rulers, elders, preacher, elderly, Matt. 5:44)
- God's will to be done, not ours (Jas. 4:13-15)
- Praise to God (Heaven, earth, Almighty, hallowed -- Psalms; Jer. 32:16-22)
- Thanksgiving to God (Life, health, country, trials, jobs, homes, ability, family, His love, forgiveness, prayer, patience, friends, material blessings, spiritual blessings, Col. 3:17; Phil. 4:6)

Of course, this is not an "exclusive" list. What other things might you include when leading a public prayer? _____
_____
_____

Mechanics In Public Prayer

Those leading public prayers are praying prayers on behalf of everyone else. When we pray, let us remember:

1. We speak loud enough to be heard! This means you must speak up and project your voice! If this means coming to the microphone to lead a prayer, then please do. In fact, this is a preferred method because folks are sure to be able to hear you when your voice is projected through the speakers.

2. We speak so all listening can say "Amen" to the prayer. Do you know what "Amen" means? _____
_____
_____

3. Prayers do not need to be eternal to be immortal.

4. This is not your personal prayer to God, but a prayer you are leading on behalf of the entire congregation. Be mindful of those you are leading in this prayer.

Some Needs In Our Prayers.

In all prayers we offer (public/private) there are some necessities that cannot be ignored. What are some of these?

We need faith (Jas. 1:6; Lk. 18:8). Someone has said that if you're praying to God for rain, then take an umbrella when you go out. Do we truly believe what we are praying and that God will listen to our prayer?

We need fervency (Jn. 4:24; Jas. 5:16). Praying *"in spirit"* certainly speaks to the fervency of prayers, just as James 5:16 teaches. Let our prayers be truly from the heart, and not some "rote" thing we say.

We need a context for our prayers. In other words, make sure they are *appropriate* for the occasion. Examples:
- When we are at home and offer a prayer at mealtime, do we generally ask the Lord to give us a good night's rest, too?
- If we are at the hospital and praying for someone who is sick. Do we generally then pray for the government as well?

Similarly, when leading prayers during the worship services, or Bible studies, etc. Let them have a context and let them have fervency! We will offer different types of prayers during the Bible study time, at the beginning of worship, the Lord's Supper, and dismissal. Let us not pray the exact prayer for every occasion.

Some Prayer Outlines

(These are suggestions, and not meant to be said by "rote." Perhaps these outlines will stir our minds up, that we might lead prayers appropriate for the situation. -JJ)

I. **PRAYER AT THE BEGINNING OF WORSHIP:**
   A. Address God
   B. Expression of Thanksgiving:
      1. For the physical ability to assemble.
      2. For the opportunity to study God's word.
      3. For salvation.
      4. For Jesus Christ's sacrifice on the cross.
   C. Requests:
      1. Wisdom for the preacher.
      2. Understanding of brethren.
      3. For growth and development as a congregation.
      4. All we do in worship will please God.
   D. Ask in Jesus' Name.
   E. Amen.

II. **DISMISSAL PRAYER:**
   A. Address God.
   B. Expression of Thanksgiving:
      1. For the opportunity to worship.
      2. For the gospel message we have heard.
      3. For the opportunity to be with brothers/sisters in Christ.
   C. Requests:
      1. For protection as we leave and go home.
      2. For spiritual strength and courage as we face the world.
      3. To overcome temptations.
      4. For God's blessings on all of us.
   D. Ask In Jesus' Name
   E. Amen.

Questions

1. What are some things we might pray for at the Lord's Table?

2. What are some things we might pray for at the beginning of services?

3. What are some things we might pray when praying for the sick?

4. What are some things we might pray for at the close of services?

"On-Your-Feet"

Be ready to practice offering a prayer at the Lord's Table.

Be ready to practice offering a prayer at the beginning of services.

Be ready to practice offering a prayer for the sick.

Be ready to practice offering a prayer for the dismissal of services.

Lesson 5:
The Lord's Supper And The Collection (Giving)

The Lord's Supper and giving of our means are two acts of worship that are to be done only upon the first day of the week (Acts 20:7; I Cor. 16:1-2). We need men available to help serve the elements and collect the funds. Our practice is that before the Lord's Supper is passed to the congregation, some words are said, or verses are read so as to prepare our minds for what we are about to do. Remember, the Lord's Supper is a memorial to the Lord's death! It demands a solemn attitude and demeanor.

What Are Things We Can Do To Help Folks In This Aspect Of Worship?

1. If you are asked to lead the thoughts at the Lord's Table, then familiarize yourself with passages which are appropriate for serving at the Lord's Table (Ex. Matt. 26:26-29; Mk. 14:22-25; Lk. 22:19-20, 29-30; I Cor. 11:23-29). Certainly, there are other appropriate Scriptures which talk about the death/sacrifice of Christ for our sins. Reading these passages and talking about their meaning will help the congregation focus their minds on the purpose of the Lord's Supper.

2. If offering a prayer for the elements of the Lord's Supper or for the giving, make sure it is appropriate for the occasion. Some brethren lead prayers, and never thank God for the bread and the fruit of the vine! (Study Matthew 26:26-27; Mark 14:22-23; and I Corinthians 11:24-25 and you will discover that to "bless" the bread or fruit of the vine means "give thanks"!)

> ## An Example Of A Prayer One Might Offer At The Lord's Table
> A. Address God.
> B. Expression of Thanksgiving:
>   1. For bread/ fruit of the vine.
>   2. For God's love.
>   3. The sacrifice of Christ.
>   4. For this supper as a reminder.
> C. Requests:
>   1. Help us control our minds to partake in an acceptable way.
>   2. A fuller understanding of what the crucifixion of Christ means.
>   3. For God's blessings.
> D. In Jesus' Name
> E. Amen.

3. Keep in mind that older folks might need help holding the tray when you hand it to them. Be considerate and do not be in a hurry! You might need to put your hand under the tray, or just hold the tray for them.

4. Remember that you have a responsibility in partaking of the Lord's Supper, too. Therefore, don't get so "caught up" in serving that you forget to focus on the Lord's death, yourself (I Cor. 11:28-29).

5. As with earlier lessons (Prayer, Reading, etc.) make sure you speak up and speak clearly so that all can hear when you offer a prayer. Similarly, if you are asked to "preside" at the table and help focus our minds, speak up! People need to hear so their minds can focus on the cross.

6. Make a clear distinction between the Lord's Supper and the giving of our means. These are two separate acts in our worship, and people need to understand this. Therefore, those who are asked to take the lead at the Lord's Table might make one of these comments:

"Having concluded the Lord's Supper, we now have the opportunity to give as we have been prospered."

OR

"The Lord's Supper is concluded. We will now take this time to give as we have been prospered."

To offer a prayer to God thanking Him for our physical blessings before the collection is entirely appropriate also (I Thess. 5:18; Col. 4:2).

Questions

1. What are the elements of the Lord's Supper?

2. What does each element represent?

3. What ought our mindset be when serving/partaking of the Lord's Supper?

4. What might be a good thing to say to help folks distinguish between the Lord's Supper and the giving?

"On-Your-Feet"

Practice a prayer for the bread.

Practice a prayer for the fruit of the vine.

Practice serving the elements.

Lesson 6:
Making A Short Talk

As a member of the congregation, from time to time, you may be called upon to make a short talk on Wednesday night, or to "fill-in" on Sunday. For this reason, we need to be prepared and take some advice that might make the occasion of speaking before a group a little easier.

Speak On A Subject That Is Familiar To You.

Don't try to speak on something you do not know or fully understand. Speak on the necessity of baptism, the Lord's church, the crucifixion of Christ, or other similar topics that are more familiar to you. It is a fact at the more familiar you are with a topic, the less nervous you will be when speaking. (Remember our lesson on "stage fright.)

More important than defeating "stage fright," I need to know the Bible and know what I intend to teach folks. In order to speak on any subject, I must ***study! study! study!*** (II Tim. 2:15; Eph. 3:4). There is no substitute for making time to study God's word daily (Ps. 1:1-2). By making time now for the study of God's word, then when the time comes that I am called to speak before the brethren I'll be ready!

Speak Out So All Can Hear You.

By now, we ought to be familiar with this need. If you're speaking the truth, then do not mumble, or talk so low or so fast that people cannot hear the truth being preached! Speak up and speak out if you are trying to teach people the truth. To do so is to follow the examples of Jesus, Philip, and Peter.

- Matthew 5:2 - *"And he opened his mouth, and taught them...."* (This is speaking of Christ)
- Acts 8:35 - *"Then Philip opened his mouth, and began at the same Scripture, and preached unto him Jesus."*
- Acts 10:33 - *"Then Peter opened his mouth, and said, Of a truth I perceive that God is no respecter of persons."*

Be Conscious Of The Power Contained In The Spoken Word.

Perhaps we take this for granted, but remember, God's Old Testament prophets ("mouths") were the ones sent to call the Jewish people back to God. In like manner, God still needs "mouths" today to tell people about His truth (Jn. 17:17). We know Christ told His apostles to *"preach the gospel"* to all men (Mk. 16:15). Paul said he endeavored to *"persuade men"* concerning the truth (II Cor. 5:11). It is through preaching the truth that men are to be saved (I Cor. 1:21).

Therefore, if we are interested in leading people to God. We want them saved, and not lost. Therefore, let us never forget the power of words *"fitly spoken"* (Prov. 25:11; Rom. 1:16-17)!

Remind Folks Of The Lord's Plan Of Salvation.

Perhaps this goes without saying, but it needs to be said. If you are planning on offering a short talk or a sermon, **always remind people of what is necessary to be saved** (Acts 2:36-38)! Don't ever assume that people already know what to do to be saved. Do not assume to know the minds of people. There are people in attendance that might not have been here in times past, but they are here now. There are people in attendance who might not have been of the mindset to listen or were not mature enough before, but now they are! We never know when the gospel will "prick the hearts" of people (Acts 2:37), and we need to make sure people know that this is the right time to come and make their lives right with God (II Cor. 6:2)!

Often, we hear men say words to the effect, "If you have a need, come forward." This is not enough. What are the "needs" one might have? If we do not specify the fact that people "need" to be saved and how to be saved, then how will they know what they "need"? Let us never be in such a hurry that we do not have time to tell folks what to do to be saved!

Note: On the next page is a list of Scriptures one might use when offering the plan of salvation in a short talk or a sermon. Feel free to use this list or use similar Scriptures from your own study. Either way, let us never neglect to tell people what to do to be saved!

> ## Memorize These Passages And Use Them When Talking About Salvation.
>
> - Hear (Romans 10:17)
> - Believe (John 8:24)
> - Repent (Luke 13:3)
> - Confess Christ (Romans 10:10)
> - Baptism (I Peter 3:21)
>
> <u>For the person who has fallen away and needs to return ...</u>
> - Repent of sins (Acts 8:22)
> - Confess sins (I John 1:9)
> - Pray for forgiveness (Acts 8:22)

Humbly Thank God For Your Ability He Has Granted You.

Everyone must thank God for their talent. If we become "puffed up," thinking that we are better than others because we have the ability to speak, then we are sure to fall (Prov. 16:18). Paul taught folks, *"In everything give thanks: for this is the will of God in Christ concerning you"* (I Thess. 5:18). How often do we thank God for the ability and opportunity to stand before God's people and lead them (in prayer, in a lesson, in song, etc.)?

Humility is a great necessity. If you don't believe this, notice that Herod was killed for not giving God the glory (Acts 12:21-23). In truth, ingratitude leads to many other sins (Rom. 1:21-32). Don't be guilty of ingratitude!

Be Ready For And Open To Criticism.

Criticism can be constructive or destructive. Do you know the difference between the two? Folks have our best interests in mind when they offer constructive criticism. Take it kindly, thank them warmly, and apply it quickly.

Some may have nothing but bad to say. In such cases, consider it (sometimes, there is truth to the criticism), and then pray that you don't become hardened or bitter to someone's harsh words.

Questions

1. When you hear someone offer an invitation, what qualities do you find helpful? Not helpful?

2. What is the final standard for determining whether or not a short talk or sermon has been successful?

3. What are some things we can do to make these talks as effective as possible?

"On-Your-Feet"

Make a short talk (invitation) from Mark 16:16.

Make a short talk (invitation) from Acts 2:38.

Have you written any short talks? Bring one and practice it in front of the class.

Conclusion

I thank you for taking part in this training program. I pray that the work you have done will help you in taking part in the various aspects of our public worship.

Remember that such lessons as these are necessary from time to time. It is good to "refresh" our memory and "sharpen" our skills as we lead folks in worship.

May our work never become "rote." May it never become merely something we "do." May we always be mindful of "who" the actual "audience" in worship is – God (Jn. 4:24)!! May we be mindful that we are the participants, helping everyone else participate in worship in a way that is *"decently and in order."*

Thank you for the work you are doing and thank you for helping us worship *"in spirit and in truth"*!

- Jarrod Jacobs

Extra Material .....

Advice When Speaking Before A Group

1. Speak so as to be heard. Remember, the people in the back of the building need to hear you! You do not have to yell but project your voice.

2. Make eye contact with the people. Don't bury your head in your notes/songbook/Bible. (Trick: Lay your notes/songbook/Bible down on the stand, and then place your index finger on the line you are reading. This allows you to look up from time to time, and you do not lose your place!)

3. When leading songs, announce the song numbers at least twice in two different ways. (Example: "Our next song will be number 418, number 4-1-8.") Or, announce the number, and then the title of the song. In this case, you might announce the song number, the title, and the number again before beginning the song.

4. Have enthusiasm as you speak/lead songs. Enthusiasm is contagious!

5. Don't put your hands in your pockets when before a group. Rest your hands comfortably at your side. (When leading songs, if you would use one hand to keep time, then this keeps one hand busy, and you're not tempted to put it in your pocket!)

Christians Sing
Jay Norris (1924-2013)

Christianity was born with a song on its lips. When Mary learned of God's favoring her with a child of the Holy Spirit, she sang praises to homes and God. Her song is recorded in Luke 1:46-55.

The night Jesus was born, the very heavens were filled with the sound of angels singing "Glory to God in the highest, and on earth peace, good will toward men" (Luke 2:14). The birth of God's Son was not announced with trumpet sound nor with the plucking of harp strings but singing.

Singing is peculiar to Christianity. Of the five major religions in the world: Buddhism, Mohammedanism, Hinduism, Shintoism, and Christianity; only Christians sing.

Christians sing "spiritual songs." Colossians 3:16 says, "Let the word of Christ dwell in you richly in all wisdom; teaching and admonishing one another in psalms and hymns and spiritual songs, singing with grace in your hearts to the Lord."

This is Holy Spirit-inspired Scripture, the word of revelation Jesus brought into the world. Paul is giving a command for obedient believers to live continually under the influence of the Spirit by letting the Word control them.

We are to live pure lives, confessing all known sins, and depending on God's power in all things. Being filled with the Spirit is living in the conscious presence of the Lord Jesus Christ, letting His mind, through the word, dominate everything that is thought and done. Being filled with the Spirit is the same as walking in the Spirit. Christ exemplified this way of life (Luke 4:1).

The Holy Spirit fills the life controlled by God's Word. This emphasizes that the filling of the Holy Spirit is not some ecstatic or emotional experience, but steady controlling of the life by obedience to the truth of God's Word.

Christians do not sing the songs of those who do not know God. Christians sing the spiritual songs that are intended to draw us closer to God. Christians sing songs that teach and admonish one another (Colossians 3:16). Christians sing songs that express gospel truth and songs that are in harmony with God's Word.

Christians sing with the sweetest melody of which the human heart is capable. We are to "sing with the spirit" (1 Cor. 14:15) which means that our songs must first come from a source much deeper than our vocal cords—the heart.

The Scriptures say, "...making melody in your hearts to the Lord: (Eph. 5:19), indicating that one person's heart may be far more "in tune" with God and His Word than another person's whose voice may be well trained and beautiful to the human ear but whose heart is "out of tune" with God and His Word. God does not care how beautifully you sing with your voice. God listens to the beauty of the heart.

We are also to "sing with the understanding" (1 Cor. 14:15) of what we are singing—that is, the words—the meaning of the songs we sing. We are not singing for the entertainment of other people but for the praise and honor of God and for the "teaching and admonishing"—the edification—of one another.

The Scriptures command Christians to sing, in general: all Christians—not just a select few. The nine passages that mention music in worship to God says, "Sing"— everyone.

Not one passage in all the New Testament regarding Christian worship to God on this earth mentions instruments of music — Not one. Nor is a choir mentioned to entertain the rest of the audience.

Furthermore, every passage that says "sing" is in the form of a command — not a suggestion. Christians are commanded to "sing." Singing is defined as "sustained speaking." Therefore, singing is not humming or whistling, though all are done using vocal cords.

Singing is sustained speaking so that Paul said, "Speaking to one another in psalms and hymns and spiritual songs, singing and making melody in your hearts to the Lord" (Eph. 5:19). All nine passages in the New Testament regarding singing seems to apply to all Christians without regard to whether they can "carry a tune." The melody is in the heart.

Singing is much more than a mere Christian "duty"; it must be our very nature as a Christian to sing. The New Testament teaches us that the word of Christ is to dwell richly within Christians, in our hearts, to overflow in song.

The New Testament teaches us that the word of God fills every Christian with the Holy Spirit of God so that singing is the very overflow of our hearts.

The Christian has a heavenly Father and a Savior who is Heaven's love-gift who died for our sins. The Christian has the hope of Heaven to make our hearts burst open into songs of praise and thanksgiving and teaching and admonishing others.

No wonder Christians sing! Think on these things (Phil. 4:8).

Made in the USA
Middletown, DE
04 May 2024

53809227R00026